BABYWATCH

An Everyday Cookbook for Babies

...6 months plus

by Ali J Burns-Hill

Babywatch

Elite Words & Image, P O Box 24, Sherborne, Dorset
Copyright © Ali J Burns-Hill, 1990
The author asserts moral rights
Professional advice should always be followed

British Library Cataloguing in Publication Data
        Burns-Hill, Ali J. (Alison Jane) 1963 –
            Babywatch.
            1. Babies. Food – Recipes
            I. Title
            641.5622

Printed in Great Britain by Stable Design and Print
Typeset in ITC Galliard
Cover illustration and line drawings by Paddy Mounter
Page layout & imagesetting by L.P. & T.S. Publishing Services

ISBN 0 9516677 0 X

Acknowledgements

I should like to express my particular gratitude to my husband, Gary, Barbara Crossley and Gilly Dibben for their support and encouragement; and, of course, my daughters who have been very patient and understanding.

Babywatch

Contents

Introduction

This book is about preparing good wholesome foods for your baby both quickly and conveniently. It also incorporates some useful dietary information for Mums or Carers with babies who have one of the more common food allergies or, possibly, a weight problem (over or under).

This is not, however, a book on nutrition, nor is it a substitute for dietary advice from your dietitian if your baby has a food allergy or specific dietary requirements. This is merely an easy recipe book for any parent, or non-parent, to pick up and prepare a delicious, wholesome meal for a baby, with or without special dietary needs, in a matter of minutes.

It must be stressed how important it is that if you suspect that your baby has a food allergy it is vital that it is investigated and diagnosed *only* by a doctor. Do not attempt to diagnose and treat a baby or small child yourself.

The recipes can be easily incorporated into any family menu – although baby's foods must, of course, be prepared and cooked separately, to avoid the seasonings we adults enjoy in our foods. Don't be put off, it can be quick, easy and convenient by preparing baby's meal alongside your own.

No one can deny how easy it is to open a jar or to mix some water into dehydrated foods for baby, but is your baby a hungry baby, as my youngest daughter was, requiring possibly the quantity of two or even three jars in a meal? It can be very expensive. Does your baby require a special diet? There are suitable variations to many recipes. Or, do you simply wish to provide baby with a good, varied diet prepared by yourself? If your answer is yes to any of these questions, read on...

How long Does It Take?

There is a star rating which will give you an idea of how long a dish will take to prepare. (It does not include cooking time, where applicable.)

		With a microwave or food processor/mixer (where appropriate)
★	under 15 minutes	☆
★★	under 30 minutes	☆☆
★★★	30 minutes plus	☆☆☆

'At a Glance'

Information for each recipe to aid in selecting the right meals for your baby.

 Vegetarian – no meat or use a soya substitute.

 Cow's Milk-Free – no dairy products, substitute Wysoy, Formula 'S' or soya milk products where dairy produce is used. Or, no milk is used in this recipe.

 Natural Fibre – high bran diets are not good for babies but natural fibre contained in fruit, vegetables and wholemeal bread for example are a wise addition to everyone's diet.

 Egg-Free – eggs are not used in this recipe. Or, use an egg replacer.

 Gluten-Free – a recipe without wheat, barley, oats or rye. Or, use a gluten-free substitute.

Babywatch

'At a Glance'

 Notably High Calorific Value – this symbol is used when the dish has a particularly high calorific value.

 Notably Low Calorific Value – this symbol is used when the dish has a significantly low calorific value.

 Pre-Cooked Meat to Save Time – using pre-cooked meat will save time in preparation but if there is none available cook from fresh.

 Suitable for the Whole Family – all the recipes in this book are suitable for the whole family with the addition of seasoning, herbs and spices but this symbol is used when no additions are necessary.

 Suitable for Freezing – can be frozen but remember to date and use quickly.

Food, Glorious Food

In the Kitchen

Kitchen Care and Utensils

All Mums, I am sure, keep a clean kitchen, but it is especially important when there is a young baby in the house and you are preparing bottle feeds and food. Here are a few hints:-

Keep your kitchen work surfaces, sink and drains scrupulously clean.

Keep your fridge clean and at the right temperature – below 5°C – fridge thermometers are available quite cheaply at hardware shops. Remember to cover all food or store in air tight containers – do not put half used cans in the fridge. Store cooked food at the top and uncooked at the bottom and watch out for leaking containers.

Always remember to wash your hands after using the toilet and changing nappies and always before handling food – use a waterproof dressing to cover any cuts or scratches.

Useful Equipment for Preparing Food

The basic equipment you will need to prepare baby's food is inexpensive – you will probably have all you need, except possibly a hand blender would be a useful addition if you don't own a food processor/blender. Alternatively a sieve can be used to push the food through.

Using a microwave is a boon to a busy Mum as it cuts cooking times drastically and makes warming food and bottles simple and mess free. It is not, however, generally recommended that you use a microwave for heating baby's bottles and foods but, if you do, remember that the milk or food will continue to cook for a minute or so after being removed from the microwave. It will also warm unevenly, so be sure to mix it well or shake the bottle well to disperse any hot spots and always check the temperature before giving it to baby. Please also note that a microwave is not suitable for sterilising a baby's bottle.

Other small pieces of equipment you might find useful are: a measuring jug which has various measuring capacities marked on it; kitchen scales; some small air tight containers for storing prepared foods in the fridge or freezer (yoghurt pots with lids are very useful for this) and possibly some ovenproof dishes.

Preparation of Meat and Vegetables

Meat and Fish

It is wise to cut up all meat into fairly small pieces and to eliminate any excess fat or gristle – wash meat and fish under cold running water before cooking.

Vegetables, Fruits, Grains and Pulses

All vegetables, fruits, grains (i.e. rice) and pulses should be washed before using or cooking. Washing should also apply to all the family's meat, fish, vegetables, fruits, grains and pulses.

Never...but always remember

NEVER ...

* add salt to baby's food
* add cereal to bottle feeds
* leave baby alone when eating
* give small sweets, nuts or toys
* reheat your baby's warmed food or bottle – all unused portions and feeds should be thrown away
* use water which has been boiled several times, water which has passed through a water softener or water from your hot tap to make up milk feeds

ALWAYS REMEMBER ...

* drinks are important – especially in warm weather
* to give baby a range of different foods to give him an interesting life!
* your baby's appetite will vary
* to talk to your Health Visitor if you have a worry – no matter how small
* that a happy and relaxed Mum will make for a happy and relaxed baby
* to check bedding and clothing for long ties or ribbons – babies can choke on long ribbons on clothes or bibs, or long ties on cot bumpers for instance

Food, Glorious Food
The Good, The Bad and The Ugly

Too Little and Too Much ...!

Fibre

Fibre is lacking in commercial baby food, as it is in most adult diets – wholemeal bread, brown rice, fresh fruits and vegetables together with plenty of fluids is a recipe for prevention of constipation as well as a healthy remedy and an integral part of healthy eating,

BUT

Babies and small children should not be fed pure bran in their diets, it can prevent absorption of vital vitamins and minerals into their body.

Salt

Salt, in baby's food, is to be avoided for at least the first year. A baby's kidneys are not mature enough to handle intakes of salt.

If you have a water softener installed in your home be sure to use the water directly from the mains supply. Water softeners often use sodium chloride (salt) in the softening process which means that the water will have a higher sodium level than in normal tap water.

Food, Glorious Food

The Good, The Bad and the Ugly

Foods to be Avoided

Meats – bacon, spam, sausages, luncheon meat, corned beef, cured tongue, salt beef, commercial meat pies and meat pastes.

Fish – shellfish (e.g. prawns), smoked fish, smoked fish roe, canned fish.

Vegetables – pickles and pickled vegetables, or eggs, and potato crisps.

Nuts – any salted or dry roasted nuts (these are dangerous as a small child can choke on a nut).

Drinks – tea, coffee, colas and fizzy drinks and squashes.

These foods should not be given to babies under one year for one or more of the following reasons:

     a) they may contain food poisoning organisms;

     b) they contain seasonings which are not advisable for a small baby;

     c) they contain large amounts of caffeine or unwanted flavourings, colourings or preservatives.

Food, Glorious Food

Food Poisoning

Washing Up Liquid
Make sure that you rinse all cooking utensils, crockery, etc., of all traces of washing up liquid, it is as important as washing your meat and vegetables before eating them. Washing up liquid is a food pollutant just like a pesticide.

Mould
Any food that shows signs of mould should be completely discarded. Just cutting away the piece containing the visible mould is not good enough, the 'roots' may have gone a lot further.

Freezing
It is dangerous to re-freeze foods which have defrosted, whether raw, cooked or packaged/processed.

Cooked and Raw Meat
Do not store cooked and raw meat together. Always place raw meat at the bottom of the fridge and cooked meats above as cross-contamination can occur.

Re-Heated Food
If you re-heat previously cooked food make sure that it is re-heated thoroughly to kill off any bacterial growth.

Food, Glorious Food

Would You Believe it...?

... 'meat' in processed foods can include up to 50% fat, skin, diaphragm, gristle, sinew and MRM (mechanically recovered meat – the meat left after a carcass has been stripped to the bone).

... a dessert labelled 'raspberry flavour' does not contain anything remotely like a raspberry, but a 'raspberry flavoured' dessert usually contains extract of the fruit.

... cheese is made with rennet (this is taken from calves stomachs when they are killed for meat). Vegetarian cheese is made from a non-animal rennet.

... up to half of some vitamins and minerals can be lost by overcooking vegetables and throwing away the water.

... many factory farmed hens are fed artificial colour to make the egg yolks more yellow.

... you should never leave bottles of milk on the doorstep, sunlight will destroy vitamin B2.

... commercial baby foods contain very few additives as most colourings, flavour enhancers and artificial sweeteners are prohibited by law. However, vitamin and mineral additives are often included as the processing can leave the natural levels in the food considerably depleted.

... cheap is not always good. Economy fish fingers and like products can be made with 'fish mince'. Fish mince contains fish skeletons (including heads) and guts together with plenty of chemical sweeteners, colours and flavour enhancers.

Food, Glorious Food

Ever Essential...Water

Water is one of life's absolute essentials, our bodies are comprised mostly of water. Water also plays an important part in the digestion and can aid in relief of constipation.

Baby's water must always be boiled and cooled before it is used. It can be kept in a covered jug which should be sterilised and rinsed when baby is very young but at about 6 months a thorough wash and rinse are all that are needed at each change of water, at least every day.

Parents also have other worries in today's water – aluminium, lead, chlorine, algae, to name but a few. Are these substances harming our young children? We know that lead is a harmful substance, even in small quantities and aluminium is now under suspicion with a possible connection to Alzheimer's Disease.

Some manufacturers of water filters claim to have the answer with inexpensive jug type filters through to very expensive reverse osmosis. Some manufacturers claim that their product is safe to use in the preparation of baby food whilst others will not recommend their use.

The main problem area seems to be that the charcoal within the filtration unit will harbour higher levels of bacteria than are present in normal tap water. This problem can, of course, be eliminated by boiling the water before drinking it. However, the concern is that the toxins produced by the bacteria may not have been destroyed.

To combat the problem of bacteria growth some fiilters have now been impregnated with a food grade quality silver. But, as it is possible for the silver to enter the water it is not recommended that the water from most types of filters is used to make up baby foods or infant formula milks.

There are, at present, no British Standards for the manufacture of water filters. If you use a water filter the manufacturer's instructions and recommendations should be followed closely.

If you feel the only option left is to give your baby bottled water please make sure that the label does not include the words, 'natural mineral water'. These natural mineral waters may contain high levels of unsuitable substances for an infant. Bottled water should still be treated as tap water and boiled before use. It should also be kept refrigerated and used within two days of opening the bottle.

Warning:

Do not use softened water to make baby's bottles or foods – it contains unacceptable levels of salt.

Breast is Best

There are many myths, prejudices and fallacies surrounding breast feeding. Here are some facts to consider:

It is not possible to manufacture a baby milk which can replicate human milk. Formula milk can only provide what is nutritionally correct for a baby. There are many properties of human milk which cannot be reproduced.

Mother's milk is – free, nutritionally perfect, totally convenient, always in adequate supply and effortless. What more can you ask? ... a flatter tummy? Breast feeding helps your uterus shrink back into position after delivery!

From baby's point of view it's – the right temperature, no waiting around, it's nice and warm cuddling up next to Mum surrounded by Mum's familiar smell and, best of all when baby's had enough to fill his tummy he can keep on sucking for a bit of comfort before dropping back off to sleep.

Don't be put off by early difficulties – remember, when baby is born it's a new game to him as well as to you. You may feel sore and bruised after a while, there are many creams on the market that can help. Or, your midwife may be of the opinion that your own milk is the best healer and soother. By all means try her method but if you don't feel that it is working for you don't be afraid to try a cream before giving up altogether. If you can persevere it is well worth it – especially in the first few months when baby wakes up at night, you'll be glad you don't have to go downstairs to warm a bottle!

Don't be misled, when breast feeding is established it is easy to wean baby off the breast slowly, without stress and most of all without pain or drugs.

Food, Glorious Food

Don't be afraid to feed your baby with the best available. Breast milk can be expressed and refrigerated or frozen so it needn't stop you having a night out or even a day or two away!

Breast milk will give your baby extra protection from disease, viral infections and allergies. The later you introduce cow's milk into the diet of a potentially allergic baby the less chance it has of developing a food related allergy.

No other form of feeding should be necessary before the age of three months.

During the first twelve months there are benefits from continuing with either breast milk, infant formula or a follow-on milk. If breast feeding your baby for a year is unacceptable to you, at least breast feed until baby starts on solids at three to four months. Then, maybe, just breast feed before he goes to bed or, if your baby is an early riser snuggle up in bed; baby can have a feed whilst you have an extra snooze!

Food, Glorious Food

When the time comes to consider formula milk here is some information on two of the more popular brands available in the shops. These are not recommendations merely guidelines.

SMA Gold/Cow & Gate Premium – have been formulated to be as close as possible to breast milk.

SMA White/Cow & Gate Plus – have more curds than whey and should take longer to digest and is therefore recommended for hungrier babies.

All of the above mentioned formulas are suitable from birth.

Wysoy/Formula 'S' – are based on soy protein and can be fed to babies from birth, and to toddlers or children who have a cow's milk allergy or a lactose intolerance. (Check with your doctor or health visitor before changing your baby's milk to a soy based milk.)

Progress – can be used for babies of 6 months plus. It has 24 times the amount of iron and 40 times the amount of Vitamin D as cow's milk, as well as recommended levels of other vitamins and minerals. It can be used all the time or as a supplement if baby is, or has been, unwell and has not been eating properly.

Healthy Alternatives and Suitable Substitutes

Healthy Alternatives

Below are listed some every day foods, all of these things are easily obtainable and cost only a few pennies more than the items they replace. The healthy alternatives can be used in all family cooking, after all they are healthy for everyone not just baby!

Oil – cold-pressed oils are best and these include: sunflower oil, safflower oil, rice oil or soya oil.

Sugar – adding sugar to baby's diet is unnecessary. Sugar is nutritionally empty. It only serves to give us calories and so is best avoided whenever possible.

As sugar cannot be avoided entirely, in baking, for example, it is best to avoid highly refined sugar beet. Golden granulated unrefined raw cane sugar is a preferable alternative. It is available at supermarkets with no preservatives, additives or colouring.

Where sugar has been added in the recipes of this book it is a minimal amount, where *some* was considered necessary. Baby's palate is educated by the person who provides the food. Why teach baby to expect sweet things? Desserts don't have to be sweet to be nice!

Flour/Bread/Pasta – when flour is required for baking try to use stoneground wholemeal. White flour is nutritionally inferior to wholemeal and may also contain chemical additives. No additives are permitted in wholemeal flour. Likewise, try to adapt to wholemeal bread and pasta – it will at least boost your fibre intake.

Eggs – it is better to use free range eggs as battery and perchery hen food can contain a colouring to make yolks more yellow and an antibiotic to prevent disease.

Always cook eggs for babies and small children to hard boiled.

Jams – try sugar-free jam – if not for yourself baby will be quite happy. Once opened, remember to keep it refrigerated.

Drinks – use natural fruit juices where possible and dilute well with previously boiled water.

Chocolate – carob is easily obtainable from supermarkets and health food stores, it comes in spread form for toast or sandwiches, a powder for cooking or making milky drinks or bar form – just like a chocolate bar!

Carob is nutritionally superior to cocoa and contains some vitamins, it has no caffeine and is lower in calories, fat content and salt.

Rice – brown rice is unpolished and is complete with its bran.

Food, Glorious Food

Versatile Soya

Soya Milk
A suitable substitute for cow's milk in most cases, although not recommended for babies and young children.

Soya Yoghurt
See the recipe and instructions in this book for making your own yoghurt – quick, cheap and easy.

Tofu
There are three forms of tofu – silken tofu, (the softest) and soft and firm tofu, the latter is like hard cheese. A highly nutritious food.

Soya Mince or Textured Vegetable Protein
A very convenient way of making a 'meaty' dinner meat-free. Suitable for Shepherd's Pie, Spaghetti Bolognese, etc. Just hydrate and use like minced beef. It is much cheaper than meat – change over completely or start by adding some to your meat dishes to make them go further!

Soybean Sprouts
These are rich in vitamins – A, B and C and are just right in salads, stir-fry or use them in casseroles.

Soya Flour
A useful substitute for cornflour as a thickener.

Soya Sauce
Made with the soya bean and wheat – a good way of seasoning – it is very salty.

Miso
Another savoury seasoning.

Food, Glorious Food

Suitable Substitutes for Cow's Milk Allergy

Milk   Wysoy (formula), and Formula 'S' (formula) are the best substitute for milk allergic/intolerant young children.

Margarine   Pure vegetable or soya margarine. (Margarines which are fortified with vitamins are preferable.)

Yoghurt   See the easy recipe and instructions for making yoghurt from soya milk.

Cheese   Soya cheese (dairy-free) is becoming more widely available – ask at your health food store.

Chocolate   There are chocolate beans and carob buttons available which are milk-free and artificial additive-free.

Food, Glorious Food

Suitable Substitutes for Gluten Allergy

Flour   Brown rice flour or millet flour are versatile alternatives for baking and cornflour as a thickener.

Pasta   Buckwheat spaghetti, rice noodles or quinoa seeds are good when a pasta or rice type accompaniment are needed.

Bread   See the recipe for gluten-free bread.

Suitable Substitutes for Egg Allergy

Whole egg replacer – for use in cakes.

Egg white replacer – for use in meringues and desserts.

Complete egg replacer – can be used to substitute eggs for binding, whisking in meringues and desserts and beaten egg in cakes.

Make Gluten-Free Bread

275 g/10 oz potato flour
225 g/8 oz brown rice flour
250 ml/½ pt hand hot water
4 tsp dried yeast
1 tsp sugar
1 tsb oil
½ tsp salt

Place the sugar and yeast into the hand hot water and leave in a warm place until a froth 1 inch deep forms.

Mix the dry ingredients in a large bowl. Add the oil and yeast and mix to a thick batter.

Oil two 1 lb loaf tins liberally and flour. Divide the dough between the tins and leave to rise for 20–30 minutes.

Bake at 230°C/ 450°F or Gas Mark 8 for 35–40 minutes.

 Preparation time

Make Cow's Milk-free Yoghurt

500 ml/1 pt soya milk (unsweetened)
2 tsp natural yoghurt (starter)
(from previous batch, or use culture
powder to start)

Bring the milk to 43–44°C. Stir in the yoghurt starter or the culture powder.

Pour into a clean, warmed thermos flask. Leave overnight.

Transfer into a clean container and refrigerate.

It will thicken slightly as it cools. Serve with suggested purée recipes, as a topping or on its own.

★ Preparation time

Food, Glorious Food
Watch Out For The Label!

Milk Allergy

Check the label of anything you buy for:

milk, butter, margarine, cream, cheese, yoghurt, skimmed milk powder, non-fat milk solids, caseinates, whey, lactalbumin or lactose.

Some foods which will contain cow's milk and cow's milk products are:

biscuits, bread and bread mixes, breakfast cereals, cakes and cake mixes, malted milk drinks, puddings and pudding mixes, ice cream, junket and custards, cream soups and sweets.

Gluten Allergy

Look out for labels which list:

flour, oats, rye, barley, wheat flour, wheat starch, gluten flour or cracked wheat, cereal filler, cereal protein, edible starch, monosodium glutamate, hydrolyzed vegetable protein or durum flour. Malt is also a hidden source of gluten.

Be careful of commercial bread and bakery as gluten-free labels are not always strictly correct.

Foods to avoid are:

biscuits, bread, breakfast cereal, cakes, some processed dairy products, puddings, soups, some processed vegetables and jams.

Food, Glorious Food

Egg Allergy

Watch out for the following on food labels:
> vitellin, ovotellin, livetin, ovomucin and albumin.

Also a special note should be made about vaccines. Some vaccines are grown on egg cultures and you should check with your doctor about a vaccine's base if there is an egg allergy.

Foods which contain egg in one form or another are:
> cakes, biscuits, pastry, batter, egg noodles and pasta, lemon curd, malted milk drink, mayonnaise, soups, puddings and mixes.

What is an Allergy?

Why do they seem to be more common today?

An allergy is when a body's immune system becomes over-sensitive and over-reacts to something a person eats, touches or breathes. These 'things' may be seen and distinguished easily or they may be invisible and unfamiliar.

To become over-sensitive to a substance you must have been previously exposed to it and when this exposure occurs again the immune system leaps into action to attack this 'foreign' substance. This over-reaction, to something which is quite innocuous to most people, is like having an illness and the body will show symptoms such as; a rash, runny nose, wheezing and coughing, stomach upset with sickness and diarrhoea and/or watery eyes. Symptoms can be many and varied.

It has been estimated that the majority of the population in developed countries suffer with an allergy causing varying degrees of inconvenience and discomfort at some time during their lives.

Science has come a long way in the last ten or twenty years; because of this allergies are more easily and accurately diagnosed than before and the allergen, or source of irritation, is becoming more easily identifiable.

Will My Baby Develop an Allergy?

The first question you should ask yourself is, "Do I have an allergy?" and then, "Does baby's father/mother have an allergy?"

The answers to these questions have a direct bearing on whether your baby is likely to suffer with an allergy. As follows:

Both parents have the same allergy	– 70% chance
Both parents have different allergies	– 45% chance
One parent has an allergy	– 20% chance
Neither parent is allergic	– 10% chance

Some parents mistakenly believe that if they ignore the problem long enough it will disappear. Unfortunately this is not a sensible approach to take. For instance, infant colic may be replaced by a food allergy and eczema may be replaced by asthma.

If you suspect that your child has an allergy do not attempt to treat it yourself. Consult your doctor.

Allergy and Allergic Reactions

General Signs of Allergy and Allergic Reactions

A baby will look and behave unwell with possibly a puffy face with dark circles around the eyes. The eyes may also be runny and sticky with a constantly runny nose.

For gastro-intestinal upsets they may have a pot belly and baby may go from diarrhoea to constipation and vice versa.

Asthma

With some asthmatics it is easy to pin-point a food which causes an attack; wheezing will start 10–15 minutes after the food has been eaten. Some common culprits are cheese, fish, nuts and fruit.

It is important for an asthmatic to avoid very heavy meals especially near bed time. An over-filled stomach will constrict the chest and cause breathing difficulties. It is also important that an asthmatic child should not become overweight as this will put extra burden on the lungs.

Eczema

The elimination of certain foodstuffs from the diet of an eczema sufferer is a little controversial because the severity of the rash can vary from day to day. In several studies it has been found that two thirds of children will show improvement in their skin condition when certain foods are eliminated. This improvement can take as long as six weeks before it is noticeable.

Allergy Aware

A baby with eczema needs to be treated with great care. If the baby is still being breast or bottle-fed then the culprit could well be cow's milk and can easily be eliminated. Cow's milk can be re-introduced with caution at about one year. If eggs are the problem you can try again at about 18 months.

Gastro-Intestinal Allergies

A gastro-intestinal allergy does not necessarily mean that a baby will always show the same symptoms. For example an American study showed that a third of children who suffered with asthma, suffered with colic as babies.

The most likely culprits for causing excessive colic in babies are cow's milk and wheat but not necessarily both.

Hyperactivity

A hyperactive baby is restless, sleeps poorly and cries a lot. Colic, eczema and allergies affecting ear, nose and throat are common.

Parents of hyperactive children should see their doctor for advice. There is also The Hyperactive Children's Support Group for which the address is given at the back of this book. If the source of the problem can be eliminated from the child's diet it can make a considerable improvement to the quality of all the family's lives.

Common Culprits for Food Allergies

Cow's milk, eggs, cheese, chocolate, wheat, fish, shellfish, nuts, peas, tomatoes, strawberries, pineapple, citrus fruits, mushrooms, yeast, spices, seasonings, food preservatives and colourings.

Allergy Testing

Three of the more common allergy tests are: the prick test, the cytotoxic test and the RAST test, these try to define a specific allergen (substance which causes a reaction).

The Prick Test

A prick is made in the skin of the arm or the upper back, through a drop of an allergen. Each prick, with each allergen, should be made with a clean needle or the results may prove the patient to be allergic to 'everything'.

When a positive result occurs it will begin with itching and then a wheal will form on the skin. A positive skin test can be misleading. It could mean that a reaction exists but not enough that it would have been noted by the patient. It may also mean that it is a past or future sensitivity.

A negative skin test can also be misleading as it may be that the skin is not capable of reacting (usually a problem in older people) or, the testing allergen may have become so weak that it is useless, or the test may not have been carried out properly.

Cytotoxic Test

A sample of blood needs to be taken from the patient. The white cells are separated and exposed to possible allergens, reactions are noted and a diagnosis made accordingly.

This test is open to a lot of controversy as its results can be very inconsistent. The results can vary from technician to technician as well as from day to day with the same patient.

Allergy Aware

RAST Test

The RAST test or Radio Allergo-Sorbent test is again done with a sample of blood taken from the patient. This time the levels of a particular antibody are measured. If the level is high then a positive result is noted. A positive result has been found to be completely reliable.

If, however, there is a negative result it could mean that levels of a different antibody are raised because of a different allergen, and this would not have been measured.

Another, perhaps, less well known allergy test is the Vegatest.

Vegatest

The Vegatest is not new but its use in allergy detection is new. It has about an 80% accuracy, is painless, can provide virtually instant diagnosis and can cover a wide range of potential allergens in a short space of time. You can even provide your own possible allergen to be tested.

The Vegatest is an electronic device which works on the basis of bio-energetics and electro-acupuncture. Your skin is not punctured with a needle, the only discomfort you may feel is where a pen-like instrument is rested on your thumb, just to the side and below your nail, which is the electro-acupuncture. The bio-energetics is the measure of your body's electrical resistance when it is challenged through the Vegatest circuit with various substances. These readings, together with some medical history, enable the trained operator to make a diagnosis.

Allergy Aware

I was tested during the research of this book. I have suffered with migraines for some years and I had had my suspicions about some foods! These were peanuts and pork. The peanuts proved to be an allergen. The pork did not register because I have not had pork in my diet for many years. There were a couple of surprises however. I love to bake and eat a carrot and cinnamon cake. I have discovered that I am allergic to both carrot and cinnamon. You often crave the foods that don't agree with you!

Some Digestive Ailments and Symptoms

Colic

Colic is when a large amount of gas has built up in baby's intestines.

It will cause extreme discomfort and constant crying. A milk allergy is the most common cause of colic. For the bottle-fed baby change to a soya based formula. For a breast-fed baby the mother should abstain from all dairy products. Elements of foods the mother eats will pass through to the baby so it is probably best if you avoid any 'gassy' types of food (highly spiced, beans and alcohol, for example).

If this does not bring some relief it could be another type of food which causes the problem. Consult your doctor.

Constipation

Mother's milk is exactly the right balance for a baby and it is, therefore, unlikely that a breast-fed baby would become constipated.

If a bottle-fed baby becomes constipated the first thing to try is to give extra water.

Consult your doctor if the constipation persists.

Crying

Crying can be caused by: hunger, tiredness or illness, dirty nappy or nappy rash, wind, colic, boredom, teething, cold or hot. A mother learns to distinguish between one cry and another but if your baby is crying more than usual it is possible that baby is unwell. Look for any other symptoms – fever, vomiting, diarrhoea or pulling at the ear. Consult your doctor.

Dehydration

This can occur when baby has been vomiting or had diarrhoea; has refused to take fluids during illness; or, has lost a lot of fluid through excessive sweating in hot weather.

Symptoms – dry mouth, drowsiness or irritability, fewer wet nappies, dark-ringed eyes, sunken fontanelle (soft-spot), baggy skin over stomach. Consult your doctor.

Diarrhoea

Nappies are filled with foul-smelling watery green or yellow stools.

Consult your doctor.

Eczema

Eczema is an allergic skin condition which is not contagious. The skin can show signs of some or all of these symptoms – dryness, itching, redness, crustiness, blisters and weeping.

Some possible causes are: it is hereditary, food allergy or allergic reaction. Certain foods, in particular milk and wheat, can cause allergic skin reactions. Or, externally, soaps and baby lotions often contain fragrance, lanolin and mineral oil which are three of the more common causes of skin allergy. Clothes washing powders can also cause allergic skin reactions. It is best to avoid biological washing powders if anyone in the family has sensitive skin. Use non-biological and avoid fabric conditioners if possible.

Pyloric Stenosis

This problem is most common within the first two months of birth and is more often found in boys than girls.

This is not, strictly speaking, a food ailment but a problem related to digestion of food.

The problem is that food is unable to pass through the stomach because of a narrowing of the muscle at the lower end of the stomach. This can be corrected by a simple operation.

Symptoms – frequent projectile vomiting, baby is continually hungry and is probably constipated.

Rash

Causes – heat, food allergy, allergic reaction or infectious fever.

Look at which areas of the body have been affected and what other symptoms there may be in order to consider possible causes.

Warning

Never leave baby to chance. If *any* symptoms persist, consult your doctor.

Natural Remedies

Natural remedies or homoeopathy are to help the patient to fight the ailment by stimulating the body's own natural healing resources. Homoeopathic remedies will not give the patient side-effects and are completely safe to take. They are especially effective for babies and children.

Homoeopathy is recognised by an Act of Parliament and the medicines can be obtained by private prescription or under the NHS through a local homoeopathic doctor. It is, however, now possible to buy most remedies from chemists and health food stores. Here are just a few remedies which parents of babies and small children may find of use:

Antimonium tartaricum – for bad effects from vaccination.

Arsenicum album– for diarrhoea with teething.

Calendula cream – for external abrasions and nappy rash.

Chamomilla – for teething infants.

Colocynth– for colic and colic which leads to diarrhoea.

A Balanced and Healthy Diet Towards a Happy, Healthy Future

Many of the principles of simple, real food have been lost in our desires for convenience, speed and taste. Highly processed foods have given us:

Convenience – open a tin, jar or box:

Speed – they need no preparation just fry, boil grill or bake:

Taste – extensive use of chemical flavours, colour, sweeteners and salt have, in some cases, made ordinary home cooked food appear bland and uninteresting.

Don't be chemical dependent for food satisfaction. Eat fresh food wherever possible and *know* that you know what you're eating!

Fresh food is high in essential vitamins and minerals and most importantly free from artificial ingredients and their potential dangers.

Educate your children's minds and stomachs by giving them fresh food. You will find that processed foods will become unpalatable, they will be pushed away in favour of 'real' food.

Useful Notes

Pre-Cooked Meats

If you use pre-cooked and cooled meat, say, from a Sunday roast here are two things to remember:

1 be sure that the vegetables are cold before blending the meat and vegetables together for keeping; and,

2 this will cut the preparation time of many dishes drastically!

Runny Versus Solid

You may find that you need to make some recipes more liquid or more solid depending on how your baby prefers his/her food – simply add to or subtract from the liquid advised in the recipe.

'Ugh ... and Umm ...'

You will soon begin to know your baby's likes and dislikes as well as the size of his/her appetite – it is probably best to start off with half quantities in each recipe until you have these things worked out!

Good or Not So Good

Within each recipe you will find that the healthy alternative is suggested – you do not have to use these but the information is given as to why it would be better to do so.

To Carers – happy cooking, and to babies – happy eating.

B·R·E·A·K·F·A·S·T

Favourite Breakfasts

Likes/Dislikes	🍦	✷	🦉	✳	✕	◀	◁	⊞	🚂	❄
French Toast	✓	✓					✓		✓	✓ ✓
Carob Breakfast Bun	✓	✓		✓	✓	✓			✓	✓
Coconut Breakfast Bun	✓	✓			✓	✓			✓	
Malt and Honey Loaf	✓	✓			✓	✓			✓	✓
Apricot Purée	✓	✓		✓	✓		✓		✓	
Baked Banana and Almond Purée	✓	✓		✓	✓		✓		✓	
Stewed Apple and Sultana Purée	✓	✓		✓	✓		✓		✓	✓
Date and Carob Purée	✓	✓	✓	✓	✓		✓		✓	✓
Fresh Fruit Mélange	✓	✓		✓	✓		✓		✓	✓
Rice 'n' Carob	✓	✓		✓	✓		✓		✓	

French Toast

1 slice of bread
1 egg
2 tsbs milk
1 tsp oil

Heat the oil in a frying pan.

Beat the egg and milk together and cut the bread into quarters.

Coat the bread with the egg and milk and place into the hot frying pan – cook until golden on both sides.

Allow to cool – jam, carob or apple and pear spread can be spread on top.

★ Preparation time

BREAKFAST

Carob Breakfast Bun

150g/5oz self-raising wholemeal flour
25g/1oz carob powder
175g/6oz margarine
175g/6oz soft dark raw cane sugar
3 eggs

Cream the margarine and sugar together until light and fluffy.

Beat the eggs together and add gradually to the margarine and sugar mixture.

Gradually sprinkle in 1 tablespoon at a time of the flour and carob mixture and fold in gently.

Then, using a spoon, divide the mixture evenly into paper cases.

Bake at 190°C/375°F/Gas Mark 5 for 15-20 minutes.

★★ Preparation time ☆

Coconut Breakfast Bun

110g/4oz self-raising wholemeal flour
75g/3oz dessicated coconut
110g/4oz margarine
110g/4oz soft dark raw cane sugar
2 eggs
55ml/2 fl oz milk

Cream the margarine and sugar together until light and fluffy.

Beat the eggs and milk together and add gradually to the margarine and sugar mixture.

Gradually sprinkle in 1 tablespoon at a time of the flour and coconut mixture and fold in gently.

Then, using a spoon, divide the mixture evenly into paper cases.

Bake at 190°C/375°F/Gas Mark 5 for 15-20 minutes or until golden.

★★ Preparation time ☆

Malt and Honey Loaf

2 tsb honey
3 tsb malt extract
75ml/3 fl oz water
175g/6oz wholemeal flour
75g/3oz sultanas
1 tsp baking powder
1 egg

Warm the honey, malt extract and water in a saucepan.

Pour onto the dry ingredients and mix.

Add the beaten egg to the mixture and mix well.

Pour the mixture into a greased and lined loaf tin.

Bake at 190°C/375°F/Gas Mark 5 for 45-60 minutes.

★ Preparation time

BREAKFAST

Apricot Purée

50g/2oz dried apricots
1 tsp raw cane sugar

Cook the apricots with enough water to cover for 15-20 minutes, until soft.

Liquidise the apricots together with the cooking liquid.

Add the sugar and allow to cool.

Mix with natural fromage frais or natural yoghurt to serve.

★★ Preparation time

Baked Banana and Almond Purée

1 banana
1 tsb ground almonds
3 drops almond essence
1 tsp lemon juice

Bake the banana in its skin at 200°C/400°F/Gas Mark 6 for 15 minutes.

Remove the skin and mash, adding the other ingredients.

Allow to cool.

Mix with natural fromage frais or natural yoghurt to serve.

★★ Preparation time

Stewed Apple and Sultana Purée

1 large cooking apple
50g/2oz sultanas
1 tsp raw cane sugar

Peel, core and chop the apple and place in a saucepan together with the other ingredients over a low heat with two tablespoons water.

Cook until a purée is formed.

Allow to cool.

Mix with natural fromage frais or natural yoghurt to serve.

★★ Preparation time

Date and Carob Purée

50g/2oz dried dates
1 tsp carob/cocoa powder
4 drops vanilla essence

Stew the dates in a little water for 10-15 minutes until soft.

Beat to a stiff purée.

Add the carob/cocoa and vanilla essence and allow to cool.

Mix with natural fromage frais or natural yoghurt to serve.

★★ Preparation time

Fresh Fruit Mèlange

1 apple
1 orange
1 banana
1 ring of pineapple
1 tsp lemon juice

Prepare all fruits straight into a blender, add the lemon juice and liquidise.

Can be served with a spoonful of natural fromage frais or natural yoghurt, or on its own.

★ Preparation time

Rice 'n' Carob

275ml/½ pt full cream milk
25g/1 oz ground rice
1 tsp carob/cocoa powder
1 tsp raw cane sugar
2 drops vanilla essence

Dissolve the carob/cocoa in a little of the cold milk. Heat the remaining milk.

Add the carob/cocoa and the ground rice to the warm milk.

Bring to the boil. Keep stirring until it begins to thicken.

Add the sugar and vanilla essence.

Allow to cool.

★★ Preparation time

D·I·N·N·E·R

Favourite Dinners

Likes/Dislikes	🍦	✖	🪆	⊗	✳	⊂	◁	▣	🧑‍🍳	❄
Turkey à la King	✓	✓	✓	✓		✓				✓
Chicken and Parsnip Dinner	✓	✓	✓	✓	✓	✓		✓		✓
Golden Chicken with Sweetcorn	✓	✓	✓	✓	✓	✓		✓		✓
Beef Stew	✓	✓	✓	✓	✓	✓		✓		✓
Spaghetti Bolognese	✓	✓	✓	✓		✓				✓
Shepherds Pie	✓	✓	✓	✓		✓				✓
Cod Mornay with Potatoes		✓	✓	✓	✓	✓		✓		✓
Vegetable Goulash	✓	✓	✓	✓	✓	✓		✓		✓
Vegetable Risotto	✓	✓	✓	✓	✓	✓		✓		✓
Ratatouille	✓	✓	✓	✓		✓				✓

Turkey à la King

10g/½ oz butter
½ onion
½ green pepper
50g/2oz mushrooms
275ml/½ pt full cream milk
1 tsp oil
1 tsb cornflour
1 piece boneless breast of turkey
110g/4oz brown rice

Cook the turkey in a covered casserole dish with the oil for 40 minutes at 200°C/400°F/Gas Mark 6, turning after 20 minutes.

Melt the butter in a saucepan and add the diced onion and diced green pepper, cook gently until soft. Add the sliced mushrooms and cook for a further 3 minutes.

Place the rice in a saucepan and cover with water by about ½ inch. Bring to the boil and allow to simmer until no water remains.

Mix the cornflour with a little of the milk and add to the saucepan together with the remainder of the milk, bring to the boil stirring constantly.

Place the chopped turkey and rice into the blender and liquidise to the required consistency and mix with the sauce.

★★★ Preparation time ☆☆

Chicken and Parsnip

2 potatoes
1 large parsnip
1 large courgette
½ onion
1 piece boneless breast of chicken

Cook the chicken in a covered casserole dish with a spoonful of oil for 40 minutes at 200°C/400°F/Gas Mark 6 turning after 20 minutes.

Peel and chop the vegetables into small pieces, cover with boiling water and cook until soft.

When both chicken and vegetables are cooked, chop the chicken into manageable pieces and place into the blender with vegetables together with some vegetable water. Liquidise to the consistency required.

★★★ Preparation time ☆☆

Golden Chicken with Sweetcorn

2 potatoes
110g/4oz peas
1 carrot
110g/4oz sweetcorn
1 tsp oil
1 piece boneless breast of chicken

Cook the chicken in a covered casserole dish with the oil, at 200°C/400°F/Gas Mark 6 for 40 minutes turning after 20 minutes.

Prepare the potato and carrot and place in a saucepan, cover with boiling water and cook until soft. Add peas and sweetcorn if fresh or frozen.

Cut the cooked chicken into manageable pieces, add to the vegetables and liquidise with some vegetable stock to the consistency required.

★★★ Preparation time ☆☆

Beef Stew

75g/3oz cooked beef
2 potatoes
1 carrot
1 parsnip
110g/4oz swede
110g/4oz peas
1 tsp oil

Prepare the vegetables and place in a saucepan, cover with boiling water and cook until soft.

When the vegetables are cooled place into a blender with the beef and liquidise to the consistency required.

 ★★ Preparation time ☆

Spaghetti Bolognese

110g/4oz wholewheat pasta
110g/4oz lean mince beef
1 tsp oil
½ onion
½ can of plum tomatoes
1 tsp tomato purée
2 tsb split red lentils

Soften the onion in the hot oil.

Add the mince and cook thoroughly for 10-15 minutes over a medium heat (drain away any excess fat which may accumulate).

Add the tomato purée and the plum tomatoes and allow to simmer for a further 10 minutes.

Place the pasta and split lentils into a saucepan and cover with boiling water. Bring to the boil and simmer for 10 minutes.

When all ingredients are cooked liquidise to the required consistency.

★★ Preparation time

Shepherds Pie

110g/4oz lean mince beef
1 tsp oil
¼ onion
1 carrot
50g/2oz peas
2 potatoes
1 tsp tomato purée

Soften the chopped onion in the hot oil.

Add the mince and cook thoroughly for 10-15 minutes over a medium heat (drain away any excess fat which may accumulate).

Add the tomato purée. Cook gently for 5 minutes.

Prepare all the vegetables into a separate saucepan, cover with boiling water and cook until soft. Reserve some vegetable stock.

Put the vegetables, mince and onions and some vegetable stock into the blender and liquidise to the consistency required.

★★ Preparation time

Cod Mornay with Potatoes

1 piece cod (fresh or frozen)
275ml/½ pt full cream milk
50g/2oz cheddar cheese
1 sliced tomato
1 tsb cornflour

Cook the cod – in a microwave or steam it.

Dissolve the cornflour in a little of the milk. Heat the remaining milk.

Add the cornflour and diced cheese to the warm milk, bring to the boil, stirring constantly.

Add the cooked fish and tomato.

Liquidise all the ingredients to the required consistency.

★★ Preparation time ☆

Vegetable Goulash

½ can red kidney beans
¼ onion
1 tsb oil
½ red pepper
½ green pepper
110g/4oz mushrooms
1 medium potato
2 tsb tomato purée
110g/4oz brown rice

Heat the oil in a large pan and add the diced onion and diced peppers, cook until soft.

Add the mushrooms and cover. Cook for about 15 minutes over a gentle heat.

Add the drained beans, tomato purée and diced potato. Allow to simmer for 30 minutes.

Place the rice in a saucepan and cover with water by about ½ inch. Bring to the boil and allow to simmer until no water remains.

When both vegetables and rice are cooked liquidise to the required consistency.

★★★ Preparation time

DINNER

Vegetable Risotto

110g/4oz brown rice
1 carrot
110g/4oz peas
110g/4oz sweetcorn
½ red pepper
150ml/¼ pt vegetable stock
(from cooking the vegetables)

Prepare and cook the carrot and pepper (and peas and sweetcorn if frozen or fresh) in some water. Reserve some vegetable stock.

Place the rice in a saucepan and cover with water by about ½ inch. Bring to the boil and allow to simmer until no water remains.

Place the rice and vegetables into the blender with some vegetable stock and liquidise to the consistency required.

★★ Preparation time

Ratatouille

½ onion
½ can plum tomatoes
½ aubergine
1 large courgette
½ red pepper
½ green pepper
1 tsp oil
1 tsp tomato purée

Soften the onion in the hot oil.

Add the diced peppers, pieces of courgette and diced aubergine and allow to cook gently, covered, for 15 minutes.

Add tomatoes and tomato purée and allow to simmer uncovered for a further 10 minutes.

Place contents of saucepan into blender and liquidise to the required consistency.

Serve with mashed potato.

★★ Preparation time

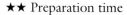

S·A·V·O·U·R·Y

Favourite Savouries

	Likes/Dislikes	🍦	🐝✕	🔥	✕	✳	◁C	◁C	▯	🤖	❄
Cauliflower Soup		✓	✓		✓	✓					
Mushrooms on Toast		✓	✓	✓	✓	✓					✓
Scrambled Eggs on Toast		✓	✓			✓					
Anellini Cheese		✓	✓		✓	✓					✓
Potato with Cheese and Onion		✓	✓		✓	✓		✓			✓
Cheese and Tomato Charlotte		✓	✓	✓	✓	✓					
Gazpacho		✓	✓	✓	✓	✓					
Courgette and Lentil Savoury		✓	✓		✓	✓					✓
Savoury Rice		✓	✓		✓						✓
Kedgeree						✓					✓

Cauliflower Soup

200g/7oz cauliflower cut into florets
570ml/1 pt full cream milk
pinch of nutmeg
50g/2oz cheese (optional)
1 level tsb cornflour

Cook the cauliflower – in a microwave or on a hob – until soft, and drain.

Dissolve the cornflour in a little milk and heat the remainder.

Add the cornflour and the diced cheese if desired, to the warm milk.

Bring to the boil, stirring constantly.

Liquidise or mash the cauliflower, add to the sauce with a pinch of nutmeg and mix.

★★ Preparation time ☆

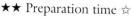

Mushrooms on Toast

¼ onion
175g/6oz mushrooms
4 pieces wholemeal toast
275ml/½ pt full cream milk

❀ ❀ ❀ ❀ ❀

Heat the milk and add the diced onion and chopped mushrooms. Bring to the boil and allow to stand whilst the toast is made.

Break the toast into the blender and make into toasted breadcrumbs.

Check that mushroom and onion are softened and add to breadcrumbs and liquidise.

Note
This recipe can be used as a tea-time spread omitting the breadcrumbs and milk for older children.

❀ ❀ ❀ ❀ ❀

★ Preparation time

Scrambled Eggs on Toast

1 tsp butter
2 eggs
2 pieces wholemeal toast
150ml/¼ pt full cream milk

Beat the eggs with 2 tablespoons of milk.

Melt the butter in a saucepan and add the beaten egg, keep stirring, over a medium heat.

Break the toast into the blender and make toasted bread-crumbs.

When the eggs are cooked add to blender with remainder of milk and liquidise to the consistency required.

★ Preparation time

Anellini Cheese

275ml/½ pt full cream milk
1 tsb cornflour
50g/2oz cheese
110g/4oz anellini pasta

Dissolve the cornflour in a little of the milk. Heat the remaining milk.

Add the cornflour and diced cheese to the warm milk, bring to the boil stirring constantly.

Cook the anellini in boiling water for 5 minutes. Drain and add to the sauce.

Liquidise if necessary.

Note
Cauliflower can be substituted for the anellini.

★ Preparation time

Potato with Cheese and Onion

2 potatoes
¼ onion
25g/1oz cheddar cheese
150ml/¼ pt full cream milk

Place the sliced potatoes and diced onion into a saucepan with the milk and bring to the boil.

Add the diced cheese whilst simmering for 5 minutes.

Pour the mixture into a lightly oiled ovenproof dish. Bake at 200°C/400°F/Gas Mark 6 for 20–25 minutes or until the potatoes are cooked and the sauce is golden.

Liquidise (or mash) to the required consistency.

★ Preparation time

Cheese and Tomato Charlotte

3 slices buttered bread
3 tomatoes
75g/3oz cheddar cheese
1 egg
275ml/½ pt full cream milk

❀ ❀ ❀ ❀ ❀

Using an ovenproof dish layer the bread and tomatoes and sprinkle each layer with grated cheese until all the ingredients are used, finishing with the cheese.

Beat the egg into the milk and pour over the bread and tomatoes.

Allow to stand for 30 minutes.

Cook at 190°C/375°F/Gas Mark 5 for 20–30 minutes.

Liquidise if required.

★ Preparation time

Gazpacho

½ can plum tomatoes
¼ onion
2 inch piece of cucumber
½ green pepper
2 slices of bread
1 tsb oil
275ml/½ pt tomato juice

Tear the bread into pieces and place into blender to make breadcrumbs.

Add the remaining ingredients and liquidise.

Chill in the freezer or freezer compartment of refrigerator for 15 minutes.

Note
Makes an ideal summer teatime savoury!

★ Preparation time

Courgette and Lentil Savoury

110g/4oz split lentils
½ onion
1 tsp oil
1 tsb tomato purée
1 large courgette

❀ ❀ ❀ ❀ ❀

Wash the lentils, place in a saucepan and cover with boiling water. Bring to the boil, cover and simmer for 15–20 minutes.

Heat the oil and cook the diced onion until soft.

Add the sliced courgettes, cook until soft.

When both the lentils and vegetables are cooked place in a blender with 1 tablespoon of tomato purée and liquidise to the consistency required.

❀ ❀ ❀ ❀ ❀

★★ Preparation time

Savoury Rice

110g/4oz brown rice
25g/1oz butter
2 tsb red split lentils
1 tsp ground almonds
25g/1oz cheese (optional)
1 tsb tomato purée
1 slice bread

❀ ❀ ❀ ❀ ❀

Put the rice and washed lentils into a saucepan and cover with water to about ½ inch above.

Bring to the boil and allow to simmer gently for about 15 minutes until firm and cooked.

Stir in the remaining ingredients (liquidise if necessary) and serve with bread.

❀ ❀ ❀ ❀ ❀

★★ Preparation time

Kedgeree

1 piece cod (fresh or frozen)
½ green or red pepper
110g/4oz sweetcorn
110g/4oz brown rice
¼ onion
275ml/½ pt water

Cook the fish – in a microwave or steam it.

Place the other ingredients in a saucepan with the water and bring to the boil. Cover and simmer on a gentle heat for 15–20 minutes or until all the water has been absorbed.

Flake the fish into pieces – remember to take out any bones.

Place the fish and the other ingredients into a blender and liquidise to the required consistency.

★★ Preparation time

D·E·S·S·E·R·T·S

Favourite Desserts

	[spoon]	[crossed whisk]	[teddy bear]	[blender]	[crossed circle]	[asterisk]	[food mixer]	[microwave]	[freezer]	[snowflake]
	Likes/Dislikes									
Custard for Babies										
Fresh Fruit Mélange	✓	✓	✓		✓	✓	✓			✓
Apricot Purée	✓	✓			✓	✓	✓			✓
Baked Banana and Almond Purée	✓	✓			✓	✓	✓			✓
Stewed Apple and Sultana Purée	✓	✓			✓	✓	✓			✓
Date and Carob Purée	✓	✓			✓	✓	✓			
Carob Pudding	✓	✓			✓	✓	✓			
Carob and Apple Smoothie	✓	✓	✓		✓	✓	✓			
Plum Mousse	✓			✓	✓	✓	✓			
Yoghurt with Lemon Jelly	✓				✓	✓	✓			
Really Real Jelly	✓	✓			✓	✓	✓			
Banana Ice Cream	✓	✓			✓	✓	✓			✓
Apricot and Almond Blancmange	✓	✓			✓	✓	✓			
Strawberry Oat Pudding	✓	✓			✓		✓			
Bread and Butter Pudding	✓	✓	✓	✓	✓	✓	✓			

Custard for Babies

1 tsb custard powder
275ml/½ pt SMA/Cow & Gate Baby Milk
1 tsp raw cane sugar

Mix the custard powder with a little of the milk.

Heat the remainder of the milk then add the custard mix. Bring to the boil, stirring constantly.

Add the raw cane sugar.

Allow to cool.

Mix with any of the suggested purées or serve on it's own.

★ Preparation time

Fresh Fruit Mèlange

1 apple
1 orange
1 banana
1 ring of pineapple
1 tsp lemon juice

Prepare all the fruits straight into a blender, add the lemon juice and liquidise to the desired consistency.

Can be served with natural fromage frais, custard or natural yoghurt to serve.

Natural fromage frais makes an excellent substitute for cream in many desserts – for older babies and the rest of the family just add a little honey if required.

★ Preparation time

Apricot Purée

50g/2oz dried apricots
1 tsp raw cane sugar

Cook the apricots with enough water to cover for 15-20 minutes until soft.

Liquidise the apricots together with the cooking liquid.

Add the raw cane sugar and allow to cool.

Mix with natural fromage frais, custard or natural yoghurt to serve.

★★ Preparation time

Baked Banana and Almond Purée

1 banana
1 tsb ground almonds
3 drops almond essence
1 tsp lemon juice

Bake the banana in its skin at 200°C/400°F/Gas Mark 6 for 15 minutes.

Remove the skin and mash, adding the other ingredients.

Allow to cool.

Mix with natural fromage frais, custard, or natural yoghurt to serve.

★★ Preparation time

DESSERT

Stewed Apple and Sultana Purée

1 large cooking apple
50g/2oz sultanas
1 tsp raw cane sugar

Peel and chop the apple and place in a saucepan together with the other ingredients over a low heat with two tablespoons water.

Cook until a purée is formed.

Allow to cool.

Mix with natural fromage frais, custard, natural yoghurt to serve.

Natural fromage frais makes an excellent substitute for cream in many desserts – for older babies and the rest of the family just add a little honey if required.

★★ Preparation time

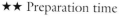

Date and Carob Purée

50g/2oz dried dates
1 tsp carob/cocoa powder
4 drops vanilla essence

Stew the dates in a little water for 10–15 minutes until soft.

Beat to a stiff purée.

Add the carob/cocoa and vanilla essence and allow to cool.

Mix with natural fromage frais, custard or natural yoghurt to serve.

★★ Preparation time

Carob Pudding

275ml/½ pt full cream milk
2 tsp carob/cocoa powder
1 tsp raw cane sugar
1 level tsb cornflour

Dissolve the cornflour and carob/cocoa into a little milk.

Heat the remainder of the milk.

Add the cornflour and carob/cocoa mixture and the raw cane sugar to the warm milk.

Bring the milk to the boil, stirring constantly.

Allow to cool.

★ Preparation time

Carob and Apple Smoothie

2 large cooking apples
2 tsp raw cane sugar
1 tsp carob powder/cocoa
3 tsb natural fromage frais

Peel core and slice the apples and cook them with a little water, until a purée is formed.

Add the sugar and carob/cocoa and allow to cool.

When cold add the fromage frais and blend well.

★★ Preparation time

Plum Mousse

1 can drained plums or 225g/8oz fresh
    eating plums
3 tsp raw cane sugar
juice of 1 lemon
275ml/½ pt double cream

Liquidise the plums, sugar and lemon juice.

Whip the cream until it peaks.

Gently fold the plum purée into the cream and refrigerate.

★ Preparation time

Yoghurt with Lemon Jelly

570ml/1 pt natural yoghurt
10g/½ oz gelatine/agar agar
juice of ½ lemon
2 tsb raw cane sugar

Dissolve the gelatine/agar agar in some hot water with the sugar.

Place the yoghurt into a bowl or container and stir in the honey and lemon juice.

Stir in the gelatine or agar agar and place into a refrigerator to set.

★ Preparation time

Really Real Jelly

450ml/¾ pt unsweetened fruit juice
1 sachet gelatine/agar agar
2 tsp raw cane sugar

Dissolve the gelatine/agar agar as per the instructions. Add the sugar and dissolve.

Stir this mixture into the juice.

Place in the refrigerator to set.

Serve with custard, fromage frais or yoghurt – or even with some Banana Ice Cream! (See recipe.)

★ Preparation time

DESSERT

Banana Ice Cream

2 large ripe bananas
150g/5oz natural yoghurt
small can evaporated milk

Blend the bananas and the yoghurt until smooth.

Put the purée into the freezer until it begins to set.

Whisk the evaporated milk until thick.

Stir the banana purée into the milk and pour into a suitable container to freeze.

★ Preparation time

DESSERT

Apricot and Almond Blancmange

50g/2oz dried apricots
275ml/½ pt full cream milk
1 level tsb cornflour
1 tsb ground almonds

Put the apricots into a saucepan, cover with boiling water, simmer for 15 minutes or until soft.

Liquidise with a little of the cooking water and add the ground almonds.

Dissolve the cornflour in a little of the milk and heat the remainder.

Add the cornflour to the milk and bring to the boil, stirring constantly.

Add the apricot and almond purée and blend.

Allow to cool and set in the refrigerator.

★★ Preparation time

DESSERT

Strawberry Oat Pudding

275ml/½ pt full cream milk
3 tsb porridge oats
110g/4oz frozen strawberries

Allow the strawberries to defrost and drain.

Heat the milk and add the porridge oats. Cook in the usual way.

Purée or mash the strawberries, add to the cold porridge oats and liquidise.

★ Preparation time

Bread and Butter Pudding

150ml/¼ pt full cream milk
1 tsb honey/raw cane sugar
1 egg
3 slices bread
50g/2oz sultanas
Sprinkling of nutmeg

❀ ❀ ❀ ❀ ❀

Begin by buttering the bread and cutting each slice in half leaving the crusts on.

Arrange the bread into a small ovenproof dish. Sprinkle the sultanas over the top.

Stir the honey or sugar into the milk.

Beat the egg in a separate cup or bowl and add to the milk. Whisk the milk and eggs together and pour over the bread and butter. Sprinkle over the nutmeg and bake in the oven at 180°C/350°F/Gas Mark 4 for about 30 minutes.

For small babies when it has cooled, liquidise and, if necessary, add some natural fromage frais or natural yoghurt to increase the liquidity.

❀ ❀ ❀ ❀ ❀

★ Preparation time

C·A·K·E·S A·N·D
C·O·O·K·I·E·S

Favourite Cakes and Cookies

Likes/ Dislikes	🍦	🚫😠	👜	⊗	✳	▲C	▽C	▦	🎪	❄
	✓✓✓✓✓✓✓✓✓✓	✓✓✓✓✓✓	✓	✓✓✓✓		✓✓✓✓✓ ✓✓✓✓			✓✓✓✓✓✓✓✓✓✓✓	✓✓✓✓ ✓

Carob Birthday Cake

Ginger and Carrot Cake

Carob Bun

Coconut Bun

Malt and Honey Loaf

Wholewheat Scones

Cookies

Carob Cookies

Ginger Cookies

Cherry Cookies

Carob Birthday Cake

225g/8oz self-raising wholemeal flour
25g/1oz carob powder
250g/9oz margarine
250g/9oz soft dark raw cane sugar
4 eggs
3 drops vanilla essence

Cream the margarine and sugar together until light and fluffy.

Beat the eggs together and add gradually to the margarine and sugar mixture.

When the eggs are blended, gradually sprinkle 1 tablespoon at a time of the flour and carob mixture and fold in gently.

Add the vanilla essence.

Divide evenly between two greased 7 inch victoria sandwich tins.

Bake at 190°C/375°F/Gas Mark 5 for approximately 30 minutes.

When cool decorate as required.

★★ Preparation time ☆

Ginger and Carrot Cake

225g/8 oz self-raising wholemeal flour
2 tsp powdered ginger
1 tsp nutmeg
½ tsb baking powder
110g/4 oz margarine
110g/4 oz honey
110g/4 oz raw cane sugar
225g/8 oz grated carrot

Sift the flour, spices and baking powder into a mixing bowl.

Melt the margarine, honey and raw cane sugar over a low heat.

Combine the melted mixture with the flour thoroughly.

Add the grated carrot.

Put the mixture into a 1 lb loaf tin and bake until firm to the touch, about 60–80 minutes at 170°C/325°F/Gas Mark 3.

★★ Preparation time

Carob Bun

150g/5oz self-raising wholemeal flour
25g/1oz carob powder
175g/6oz margarine
175g/6oz soft dark raw cane sugar
3 eggs

Cream the margarine and sugar together until light and fluffy.

Beat the eggs together and add gradually to the margarine and sugar mixture.

Gradually sprinkle in 1 tablespoon at a time of the flour and carob mixture and fold in gently.

Then, using a spoon, divide the mixture evenly into paper cases.

Bake at 190°C/375°F/Gas Mark 5 for 15-20 minutes.

★★ Preparation time ☆

Coconut Bun

110g/4oz self-raising wholemeal flour
75g/3oz dessicated coconut
110g/4oz margarine
110g/4oz soft dark raw cane sugar
2 eggs
55ml/2 fl oz milk

Cream the margarine and sugar together until light and fluffy.

Beat the eggs and milk together and add gradually to the margarine and sugar mixture.

Gradually sprinkle in 1 tablespoon at a time of the flour and coconut mixture and fold in gently.

Then, using a spoon, divide the mixture evenly into paper cases.

Bake at 190°C/375°F/Gas Mark 5 for 15-20 minutes or until golden.

★★ Preparation time ☆

Malt and Honey Loaf

2 tsb honey
3 tsb malt extract
75ml/3 fl oz water
175g/6oz wholemeal flour
75g/3oz sultanas
1 tsp baking powder
1 egg

Warm the honey, malt extract and water in a saucepan.

Pour onto the dry ingredients and mix.

Add the beaten egg to the mixture and mix well.

Pour the mixture into a greased and lined loaf tin. Bake at 190°C/375°F/Gas Mark 5 for 45-60 minutes.

★ Preparation time

CAKES AND COOKIES

Wholewheat Scones

75g/3 oz wholewheat flour
75g/3 oz self-raising flour
1 tsp baking powder
½ tsp nutmeg
25g/1 oz raw cane sugar
25g/1 oz margarine
1 egg
2 – 3 tsb milk

❀ ❀ ❀ ❀ ❀

Sift the flour, baking powder, nutmeg and sugar. Rub in the margarine.

Beat the egg and the milk together and add to the mixture.

Mix to a smooth dough to roll out to ¾ inch thick.

Cut out the scones and place them on a well-greased baking tray.

Bake until golden at 230°C/450°F/Gas Mark 8 for 15–20 minutes.

❀ ❀ ❀ ❀ ❀

★★ Preparation time

Cookies

225g/8oz plain wholemeal flour
1 tsp baking powder
110g/4oz butter
175g/6oz raw cane sugar
1 tsp vanilla essence
1 egg

Rub the butter into the flour and baking powder until the mixture resembles breadcrumbs.

Add the sugar, vanilla essence and beaten egg, mix to a smooth dough.

Turn out onto a floured surface and knead for 2 minutes.

Wrap in foil or cling film and chill for 15 minutes.

When chilled, roll flat and cut into shapes.

Place on a greased baking sheet and bake at 190°C/375°F/ Gas Mark 5 for 10 minutes or until golden.

★★★ Preparation time ☆☆

Carob Cookies

225g/8oz plain wholemeal flour
1 tsp baking powder
110g/4oz butter
175g/6oz raw cane sugar
50g/2oz carob/cocoa powder
1 tsp vanilla essence
1 egg

Rub the butter into the flour and baking powder until the mixture resembles breadcrumbs.

Add the sugar, carob/cocoa, vanilla essence and beaten egg, mix to a smooth dough.

Turn out onto a floured surface and knead for 2 minutes.

Wrap in foil or cling film and chill for 15 minutes.

When chilled, roll flat and cut into shapes.

Place on a greased baking sheet and bake at 190°C/375°F/ Gas Mark 5 for 10 minutes.

★★★ Preparation time ☆☆

Ginger Cookies

225g/8oz plain wholemeal flour
1 tsp baking powder
110g/4oz butter
175g/6oz raw cane sugar
2 tsp ground ginger
1 egg

Rub the butter into the flour, ginger and baking powder. Do this until the mixture resembles breadcrumbs.

Add the sugar and beaten egg and mix to a smooth dough.

Turn out onto a floured surface and knead for 2 minutes.

Wrap in foil or cling film and chill for 15 minutes.

When chilled, roll flat and cut into shapes.

Place on a greased baking sheet and bake at 190°C/375°F/ Gas Mark 5 for 10 minutes.

★★★ Preparation time ☆☆

Cherry Cookies

225g/8oz plain wholemeal flour
1 tsp baking powder
110g/4oz butter
175g/6oz raw cane sugar
50g/2oz glacé cherries
1 tsp vanilla essence
1 egg

Rub the butter into the flour and baking powder until the mixture resembles breadcrumbs.

Add the sugar, finely chopped glacé cherries, vanilla essence and beaten egg, mix to a smooth dough.

Turn out onto a floured surface and knead for 2 minutes.

Wrap in foil or cling film and chill for 15 minutes.

When chilled, roll flat and cut into shapes.

Place on a greased baking sheet and bake at 190°C/375°F/ Gas Mark 5 for 10 minutes or until golden.

★★★ Preparation time ☆☆

Babywatch

Useful Addresses

ACTION AGAINST ALLERGY
Greyhound House
23-24 George Street
Richmond
Surrey
TW9 1JY

FOOD & CHEMICAL ALLERGY ASSOCIATION
27 Ferringham Lane
Ferring
West Sussex

NATIONAL SOCIETY FOR RESEARCH INTO ALLERGY
PO Box 45
Hinckley
Leicestershire
LE10 1JY

ASTHMA SOCIETY
300 Upper Street
London
N1 2XX

NATIONAL ECZEMA SOCIETY
Tavistock House East
Tavistock Square
London
WC1H 9SR

HYPERACTIVE CHILDREN SUPPORT GROUP
71 Whyke Lane
Chichester
West Sussex
PL19 2LD

Babywatch

Useful Addresses

Foods and Allergy Testing
FOODWATCH INTERNATIONAL
Butts Pond Industrial Estate
Sturminster Newton
Dorset
DT10 1AZ

Allergy Testing
THE BREAKSPEAR HOSPITAL
High Street
Abbots Langley
Herts
WD5 0PU

General
CRY-SIS SUPPORT GROUP
BM Cry-sis
London
WC1N 3XX

HOMOEOPATHIC DEVELOPMENT FOUNDATION
Harcourt House
19A Cavendish Square
London
WC1M 9AD

SOYA MILK INFORMATION BUREAU
The Chestnuts
Fosse Way
Moreton Morrell
Warwickshire
CV35 9DE